Published by
Princeton Architectural Press
37 East Seventh Street
New York, NY 10003

For a catalog of books published by
Princeton Architectural Press, call toll free
1.800.722.6657 or visit www.papress.com

First published by V+K Publishing,
Blaricum, The Netherlands

© 1999 Princeton Architectural Press
03 02 01 00 99   5 4 3 2 1 First Edition

Printed and bound in The Singapore

*Library of Congress Cataloging-in-Publication
Data for this title is available from the
publisher.*

ISBN 1-56898-212-7

Design
Cees de Jong
Jeannette van Haarlem
V+K Design, Blaricum

Photography
Tim Killiam, Amsterdam

Historical photographic material
Centraal Museum, Utrecht
Bertus Mulder, Utrecht

Lithographs
Slenderprint, Ede

Printed by
Kunstdrukkerij Mercurius,
Wormerveer

Translated by
Lynn George, Norfolk

Contents

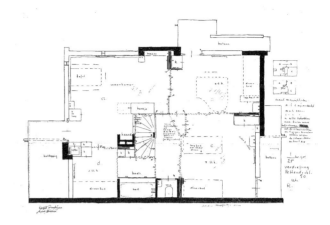

Rietveld's
design for the
system of slid-
ing partitions in
which he also
shows how the
various spaces
can be com-
bined with each
other.

Foreword

On 4 April 1987 the Rietveld Schröder House was opened to the public. This important cultural icon was initiated by Truus Schröder-Schräder, who around 60 years earlier had commissioned Rietveld to build a house for her. She was one of the first to recognise his talent as an architect and the design evolved from an intense collaboration between client and architect.

In later years Schröder realised that Rietveld's significance as part of the modern movement would be under threat if his most important work was not conserved. When the first Rietveld exhibition was held in the Centraal Museum Utrecht in 1958, she had some of the later alterations to the house removed. In 1970 she created the Rietveld Schröder House Foundation, whose task it was to safeguard Rietveld's work for prosperity and to underline the importance of his œuvre and ideas. The extensive archive, amassed by Schröder, together with the house itself forms a solid basis for this idea.

In 1975 the Foundation commissioned Bertus Mulder to restore the outside of the house. After Schröder's death in 1985 the interior and exterior were again taken in hand and this latter restoration produced a wealth of data. For this publication Bertus Mulder has set down on paper every detail he could remember about the house.

When the work was completed, the Foundation gave control of the house to the Centraal Museum. The expectation that the museum would best be able to achieve the Foundation's objective has been realised. In the last decade some 100,000 people from over 50 different countries have visited the house. The house has withstood this interest in every sense of the word. Rietveld's international reputation has increased among a wider public by the many activities generated by the museum with respect to the house, the Rietveld Schröder Archive and the Rietveld collection of furniture. The Centraal Museum considers the house to be one of the highlights of its collection and for the future deems that its access to the public, as well as other activities within the context of the Foundation's objective, are among its principle duties.

Ida van Zijl
Assistant director,
curator applied arts,
Centraal Museum

Rietveld's first maquette of the Rietveld Schröder house.

The house faced an open polder area that was situated at a lower level than the buildings of the town.

Bertus Mulder

The design

Truus Schröder
at the time the
house was being
built.

The wardrobe in
the hall of the
ground floor.
The ceiling of
the study is visi-
ble through the
upper window.

6 The Rietveld Schröder House is partly named after Truus Schröder-Schräder who commissioned Gerrit Thomas Rietveld to build a home for her in 1924. Together they created the design when Truus Schröder was 35 years old. She had a 12 year-old son, Binnert, and two daughters, Marjan and Hanneke, aged 11 and 6. Rietveld was 36 at the time. Schröder had been living with her family in a large prominent house on Biltstraat in Utrecht, which was also the premises for her lawyer husband's practice. When her husband died in 1923 after a prolonged illness, she was unable to remain living in such a big house. She considered renting something for a while as she wanted to get away from Utrecht as soon as possible. When her son had finished primary school she intended to move to Amsterdam to be nearer to her older sis-ter An. An Harrenstein-Schräder inhabited a liberal world of artists and intellectuals and Schröder sought Rietveld's help in finding her a house, which after a few minor changes, might be suitable for her and the children. She had confidence in Rietveld's ability as he had already created a room for her in the house on Biltstraat so that she had her own space in such a huge place where she never felt at home. At the time Rietveld had sensed what was needed and she was extremely happy with the result. She had also discovered they were kindred spirits searching for a new pro-gressive way of living.

As neither were able to find a suitable dwelling to rent, Rietveld suggested building one. Schröder felt that owning a house would tie her to Utrecht, but Rietveld pointed out she could always sell it when she wanted to leave. Embracing the idea, she suggested to Rietveld that a piece of land be found. They both found the same piece of ground over the same weekend. A piece of land remaining at the end of Prins Hendriklaan where four dwellings had been built. This avenue was on the fringes of town and the empty polder area. In fact the house on the other side of the avenue is still known today as 'Stadsrand' (Town Fringe). The building site was bound on the northwest side by the broad, high gable of the four dwellings, but was open on the three other sides.

The two having decided this was to be the place, Rietveld set to work immediately. He had already designed one or two extensions but never an entirely new house. He quickly came up with a proposal but it was not what Schröder envis-aged. Together they searched for solutions, using her various ideas on how she wanted to live as a starting point. First of all, she had absolutely no intention of living on the ground floor – judging it too restricted. Schröder had vivid mem-ories of walks she took as a child with her father in all kinds of weather. She wanted a house in which she could dis-tance herself from the ground in order to be closer to light, sun, wind and rain. She wanted to experience consciously the changes of nature from within her own house. She had once minded a baby of a friend who lived in a large empty attic, which appealed to her immensely, and she had tried to imagine what it would be like to live that way. The mem-ory inspired her, as she felt that life should be transparent and elementary, and 'elementary' to her was the core that emerged after the superfluous was peeled away. Schröder had been preoccupied for some time with the process of dis-

tancing herself from too many possessions and meaningless routines. She had already discovered that rationality was her life's essence. This soberness gave her the freedom to live from within. She didn't want a house that imposed a specific lifestyle on her, but rather a space in which she could develop her craving for freedom and independence. These were ideas that greatly appealed to Rietveld.

They began by designing the layout for the first floor with rooms for the children, herself, the family in general plus a bathroom and WC. Everything was carefully sited, taking into account the view, the aspect and practicalities, about which Schröder had very definite ideas. When everything was precisely in place, Schröder asked Rietveld whether it was possible to remove the walls of the rooms. 'By all means', was the reply and thus a single huge space with sitting and sleeping areas was created. After this act of 'peeling away', she still wanted the flexibility to rearrange the space if she so wished. Rietveld came up with an ingenious system of sliding walls which could be variously combined into different areas when needed. In this way an entire living space was created on the first floor, with the exception of the kitchen, which was sited on the ground floor directly under the sitting/dining area and connected by a dumbwaiter. The kitchen was intended to be a real workspace with sink and draining board, a cooker, dishwasher and a washing trough. An area, in fact, with an entirely different character and function than the open-plan living space above and the reason for separating the two. Moreover, in dealing with tradespeople, who still delivered everything to the house at the time, it was practical that the kitchen could be reached directly from the outside. A facility for leaving groceries and other deliveries was therefore designed. The ground floor also had a vestibule, a hall with staircase, a WC and three rooms planned. The space behind the kitchen was intended for the hired domestic help and beneath this was the cellar, reached by way of the kitchen. A room next to the hall was laid out as a study into which anyone unable to find sufficient peace upstairs could retreat. Schröder believed that everyone in future would have a car which simply couldn't be left on the street. The third room was therefore originally intended as a garage though this was never realised and it was used as a workroom. The hall and front door was situated on the southeast side and not on Prins Hendriklaan. According to the town plan of the time, it was intended that Laan van Minsweerd (an avenue) would be extended beyond Prins Hendriklaan, so the entrance was sited on the proposed new part of Laan van Minsweerd. Thus the house deliberately faces away from Prins Hendriklaan, an avenue which Truus Scröder and Rietveld dismissed as 'bourgeois'. However, the extension to Laan van Minsweerd was never carried out.

When the ground plans were ready, Rietveld set about designing the exterior, using a model to demonstrate to Schröder how he thought the house might look. The model already had a skylight as it was evident from the outset that light should not only enter from the sides of the house but also from above. The chimney, however, is not yet in place. But Schröder was unimpressed with the design and clearly made her feelings known. Rietveld realised that he had underestimated his client and her response inspired him to continue. He told her he thought he could come up with something better and disappeared. A little later he returned with a sketch that showed a real breakthrough. The original model was simply a rectangular box with openings totally dominated by the volumes. Only in one corner had these volumes been broken up by a large window linking the inside with the outside. The sketch, on the other hand, shows a series of horizontal and vertical elements that envelop the indoor/outdoor transitions. In the centre of the building is a rooftop glass construction that included the chimney. The plan instantly appealed to Schröder, and Rietveld worked it out in greater detail before submitting it to the local council for planning approval.

The sketch submitted for planning permission failed to indicate the presence of sliding walls on the first floor as this was against current building regulations. Instead the word 'attic' was inscribed. Because the ground floor, according to building regulations, had the requisite number of spaces to constitute a house, the layout of the first floor could be omitted. Moreover, in the side elevation the side wall of the existing block of dwellings that projects above the house has been somewhat emphatically drawn in, thereby creating an impression that the house has a slanting roof. Schröder thought Rietveld had done this deliberately to mislead the planning officials on the true form of the house. Notwithstanding, planning permission was granted without any confining restrictions.

8

South east view of the house as it is today.

The drop-off facility from the inside of the house. Above the cupboard a central-heating pipe and the speaking tube.

The sink unit on the ground floor with, above, a transparent unit for tableware. Next to the unit is the dishwasher.

The windows of the sitting/dining area. Part of a corner of the house disappears when the windows are opened.

The enlarged shopfront-type window of the study on the ground floor of Prins Hendriklaan, used to display päintings that Truus Schröder tried to sell for her artist friends.

The construction

The sketch Rietveld submitted for planning permission, drawn on a scale of 1:100 and dated 2 July 1924, was also the specification used by the contractor and more or less conforms to what was actually built. He added further written instructions to this, as well as making an extra 23 drawings for the building's execution on a scale of 1:25 and 1:10. These scales betray Rietveld's furniture-making origins for 1:20 and 1:1 scales were the norm for buildings. This is also apparent from his drawing style. He drew the aspects and cross-sections of the windows through each other, while architects usually placed these next to each other. The drawings diverge on a number of points from what was built. The sitting/dining area, for instance, on the first floor showed windows that opened outwards and which were pulled up again by a steel cable across a pulley. In reality rotating windows were made. The detailed design of various elements was only finally decided during the building process. Rietveld would make a sketch on a piece of card or a plank of wood, as became his practice with most of his later buildings. His specifications describing all the materials to be used was quite detailed. For instance, the vertical walls on the outside were to be plastered in three different grey tones, while several exterior walls were to be whitewashed with chalk. Two benches are also specified in the drawing: one in the vestibule and one in the living room next to it. Both, however, were not realised, neither does the dumbwaiter go down to the cellar as in the original specification. It was also specified that the wooden floors should remain natural. Rietveld stressed that at certain points in the building every element must fit seamlessly together. Corners in the plasterwork had to be 'square'; the roof protrusions must be flat 'square' planking, in other words minus the usual mouldings. The woodwork for the doors and windows is also specified as 'square' and without mouldings, while the lining up of windows and masonery had to be 'simple', without additions or decoration of any kind. This meant that everything had to line up properly first time and any disparities could not be corrected with final finishing touches. This was not easy to achieve.

Rietveld originally wanted to make the house from concrete and also had in mind concrete sections that could be assembled on the spot. The final design was also based on this and consists of a series of concrete components. Such a system of construction, however, was too complicated and expensive for such a small building. For this reason most of the house is built in the traditional style of the day. Only the foundations and balconies made of reinforced concrete. The brickwork of the wall elements and chimney is plastered on all sides. The window frames and doors are of wood, the floors are supported by wooden beams covered with wood planks and the ceilings are of reed and plaster. With the first floor having no walls to support the ceiling, Rietveld inserted steel girders into the flat roof. Where these girders are unable to rest on an outside wall, they are supported by steel columns. Steel girders packed in wire mesh are also used for large spans of masonry. This mesh has been plastered along with the walls so that the girders remain invisible. The steel posts in the windows and the steel balcony constructions, however, were deliberately left exposed.

Materials used

16 The kitchen with the rear door to the terrace and, left of this, the dumbwaiter. Next to this is the door of the domestic help's room. Those areas of the kitchen that could quickly become dirty were painted in darker tones of black and blue.

The door on the landing slides open by pushing down the red, wooden bobbin to the right which is linked to a rope running across a pulley.

The rooms on the ground floor merge into each other via the windows under the ceiling.

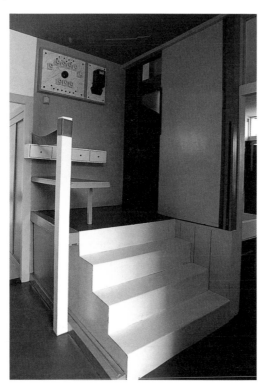

Completely new forms had to be fashioned from largely traditional building materials and the artisans had to adapt to what was for them an entirely new work experience. They were meant to study carefully how and where the idiosyncratic window frames had to be positioned; nothing was straightforward. Sometimes they deliberately inserted a frame upside down or on its side to see whether Rietveld noticed. Whenever he was not around, things sometimes went wrong. When the blacksmith arrived to install the angle iron rails for the balcony, he was uncertain how to weld them to the steel columns. He, himself, would have chosen the most obvious method of welding the flat upright side of the angle iron to the flat side of the column. This was the most simple and robust approach. He was, however, aware that everything in this house was done differently and he therefore turned the angle iron around and welded the end of the horizonal flat side to the column. Fearing that this was not strong enough, he filled the space between the angle iron and the column, thereby making matters worse. When Rietveld saw the result he left it as it was, knowing that the man had done his best.

The house is a balanced, asymmetrical and three-dimensional composition with horizontal and vertical planes and lines. No single element has been allowed to dominate the building. That is why the flat roof is only partly invisible and was made to disappear behind the outer walls that project above it. This meant the roof had to be watertight where it meets the plasterwork of the rear exterior walls, which was difficult to achieve with the materials available at the time and this has always been a vulnerable aspect of the house.

18   All the external window frames, except for one, are asymmetrical and connect at various points with the outer walls in a striking way. Some of the posts and sills are invisible where they have been imbedded into the plasterwork. The sitting/dining area on the first floor boasts the largest windows overlooking the broad sweep of the still unspoilt Johanna polder. The windows were interrupted by two steel columns that supported the roof. Schröder felt that the columns conveyed too vertical an effect, preferring the whole to be more horizontal or 'earthly', as she put it. Thus Rietveld had wooden posts made in the columns thus creating the impression that the horizontal line of the window frames runs through the columns.

In contrast to the first storey, the layout of the ground floor was fixed and in keeping with the prescribed spaces of residential building regulations. The spaces are separated by brick walls, but, apart from the workroom wall, they do not go up to the ceiling. Instead the upper part gives way to skylights, giving the impression that the ceiling is a continuation. This effect is heightened by the composition and colours of the ceilings in the hall and small study as well as the way in which the ceiling lighting has been installed. In this way even the more traditional layout of the ground floor creates an open and spacious impression.

As an integral part of the play of lines and planes of the house, the slabs for the balconies could not appear too massive so concrete was the only solution. Steel beams were imbedded into the slabs, which run into the wooden floor inside and are secured by bolts to the supporting beams. The upstairs floor is also a network of hot water pipes, which lie in channels made from planks with raised sides of board and filled with sawdust for insulation.

The interior and exterior spaces of the house are separated from each other in certain places by sections of thick wall but naturally at other points where the windows are sited. The indoor/outdoor impression is heightened on the ground floor by the projecting balconies, and on the first floor by the roof projections. The transition is made evident when the huge windows and outer doors are opened. The effect in the living area where the corner of the house is resolved is quite spectacular. All the living areas, apart from Schröder's bedroom, have an outer door. There are a total of eight such doors. It is also possible to go onto the roof via the skylight and for tradespeople to deliver provisions to the kitchen from outside via a drop-off facility.

The large window in the downstairs room on the Prins Hendriklaan is projected from the wall of the building and was initially used to display the paintings, among others, of Bart van der Leck and Jacob Bendien, which Schröder attempted to sell.

A round ventilation grille was installed above the balcony doors of her son's room, after it was realised that in this corner of the house this was the only place practical. It is round because a rectangular form would infringe too much upon the autonomy of the wall into which it has been incorporated.

The sitting area with a dropleaf table in front of the study window on the ground floor. On the other side of the wall, outside, is the blue bench.

ceiling effect

As the specification shows, Rietveld wanted several outer walls painted in different tones of grey by adding colour to the wet plaster. This, however, did not happened as he intended. He also stipulated that certain wall surfaces must have a whitewash distemper. He attempted to arrive at grey tones by mixing pigment with the whitewash and distempering all the surfaces. By so doing he achieved the desired shades of colour but it looked extremely patchy after rain as chalk is highly absorbent. Later, special wall paints were developed for outdoors. At first these were casein emulsion paints and then plastic emulsion paints were used. Both produced better results. The house was regularly re-painted under Rietveld's supervision and he always determined the colours. For the greys he mixed white and black with a little ochre and a hint of red. Initially these greys had ochre overtones, but later they became increasingly more blue. The differences in tones diminished over time. Nowdays the wall surfaces are painted in white and five different shades of grey. The window frames and doors in the openings between the sections of wall are subordinate to the colour scheme and are generally painted black. Only where certain parts of window frames project are they painted red, blue or yellow. The steel columns, beams and balcony rails are also generally black aside from the column on the Prins Hendriklaan and the recess in the columns of the window of the sitting/dining area, which are painted yellow and blue respectively. The colour provides an accent and is only applied to linear elements.

20

colors used

The small ladder used to reach the roof from inside has special iron supports so that it can be placed on top of the bannister. Directly underneath is a bar so that the sliding door to the hall can be moved from the upper floor. On the lowest rail of the bannister is the hook for securing the bar.

The stairway with the ladder in place to climb to the lowered hatch.

The interior

22 When Truus Schröder moved to the house with her children around New Year's Eve 1924, it was far from ready. The place was empty, cold and damp and had to be heated with a pot-bellied stove as the piped heating had not yet been installed. On the upper floor was a work bench where much of the interior had still to be made. This was undertaken by Gerard van de Groenekan, who worked for Rietveld as a furniture maker. He also slept in the house, much to the relief of Schröder who was still felt ill at ease in a house that was open on all sides. She began life in the new house with a clean slate. She had only taken one or two items with her from the old house: a gas heater, a bathtub, a roll of linoleum and one single chair. Like Rietveld, she wanted the house and the furnishings to form a unified whole. She also wanted the house to be put to many uses. Every room, especially on the ground floor, had to have water, electricity and cooking facilities so that anyone could live in any part of the house. Thus every space has a washbasin, enamel cast iron ones in the children's rooms and WCs, glazed earthenware sinks elsewhere. On the first floor several cupboards were made. Between Schröder's bedroom and the living area a combination of cupboards were made for under the washbasin, for crockery and for the small built-in dumbwaiter. Behind the chimneypiece is a cupboard with one section of shelves serving the bathroom and another serving the bedroom. Between the sitting/dining area and the son's room is a wardrobe with drawers beneath and a place to hang clothes above, while between the son's and the girls' rooms is a corner cupboard, part of which has floor to ceiling shelves and a lower section for use as a wardrobe. In the sitting/dining area is a modular cupboard comprising a vertical cupboard for storing taller items next to a box-like structure, the upper part of which partly folds back for the family film projector, and above that a similar box with a gramophone. To use the latter, the box is pulled forward and the lid folds back. Above this in a construction of wooden slats are three separate smaller boxes for storing writing and sewing materials, etc, which can be carried to the place of intended use. The irregular shape of the cupboard is held together by a post on the side and what appears to be a floating shelf on the upper side. In the son's room a low cupboard was made at right angles to the exterior wall where it also creates recesses for the bed and washbasin. In the living space is another low cupboard next to the sink that was used for serving food and drink.

The built-in cupboards have been so made that the sliding walls can be parked behind them when the floor is used as one large space. Rietveld designed a series of sliding walls for the first floor in such a way that a separate landing, bathroom and four rooms could be created as well as making various other combinations possible with two adjoining and interconnecting spaces. The door in the section of the sliding wall between the living area and the son's room blocks off the side of the cupboard when it is in a stationary position, as well as the light switch. In order to use this a circular opening was made in the sliding wall. The system of sliding walls was very simply constructed. The wall elements comprise a wooden framework covered on both sides with board. The space in between is filled with sheets of

The upper floor in use as a Montessori infants' school.

The sitting/dining area on the upper floor with worktops in front of the window with all the essentials the Schröder children might need to complete their school homework.

24 The open corner
window of the
sitting/dining
area.
The area
between the sit-
ting/dining area
and the son's
room with the
wardrobe unit
and pushed
back sliding
doors. The
opening in a
panel of one of
the sliding
doors shows
there was once
a switch. Now
there is a
folding mirror
behind and the
switch is in the
cupboard.

cork for sound insulation. The walls slide along metal rails attached to the floor and on the upper side in steel T-sections screwed onto the ceiling. The revolving elements are connected to the sliding ones with standard door hinges. When the sections are pulled out there are chinks on all sides which means the soundproofing does not function properly, however, these sliding walls were chiefly intended to give certain areas more privacy.

The sitting/dining area can be separated from the stairwell area with closed plywood partitions and windows in the stair railings. These are stored in front of the chimneypiece. The partitions and windows comprise two parts. One part of the partition slides into the stair railings while the other part can be folded out. One section of the windows also folds out while the other part slides along a rail on the stair railings. In order to adjust light entering the stairwell from above a wooden trapdoor can be lowered using a rope across a pulley. It is also possible to go onto the roof from the inside via the trapdoor by leaving this partly folded back. A set of wooden steps stored under the top of the dumbwaiter is then placed in front of the stair railings, while a small ladder is taken from its place against the chimneypiece and placed on the stair railings. There are special brackets on the underside for this purpose. In this way it is possible to reach the wooden trapdoor and to get onto the roof outside through a door in the skylight. The part of the trapdoor that remains folded back in order to get onto the roof can be closed from above and then you have a small attic quite separate from the rest of the house. This provided the Schröder children with a splendid space to play in a small glass house of their own. The roof can also be reached from outside via a steel ladder on the south east facing balcony.

The windows and the glass openings in the outer doors of the study, kitchen, domestic help's room and those of the children can be screened on the inside with wooden shutters. These also have a fixed place when not in use and are part of the total spatial composition. The shutters in the ground-floor doors are secured with hinges, as is the case in the daughters' room. The shutter in front of the study window is the same height and colour as the adjoining wall. The shutters before the kitchen windows are the same size as the cupboard where they are stored and those in the son's room also have special places. The shutter in front of the large glass opening in the balcony doors is unobtrusively stored behind the bed, being the same size and colour as the wall panelling. The shutter for the smaller glass opening in the balcony doors has a fixed place on a wall partition and is painted in a contrasting colour, while the partition in front of the window blocks off the mirror above the washstand. The lower part of the windows in the living area can be screened with roller blinds. There were probably blinds in the daughters' rooms, but this is difficult to establish from old photographs.

Schröder made much of being able to control on a day-to-day basis the space and light entering her environment. She chose an active way of living and unlike Rietveld was extremely driven about operating the sliding walls.

At the time houses were centrally heated with cast iron column radiators, something Schröder dismissed because of their vertical appearance. Instead, special heating elements were made from the steel pipes that were also used in workshops and factories. This seemed a simple solution but was expensive to carry out. The steel expansion tank of the heating system hangs in Schröder's bedroom, while the boiler – originally stoked with coal and later fitted with an oil burner – is in the cellar. During less cold weather the upper floor was heated with a gas fire taken from the old family home on Biltstraat.

The gas fire appears in photographs taken of the room there that Rietveld first desgined for Truus Schröder. During the war the gas fire was replaced by a stove that was suitable for any type of fuel.

Schröder considered the stone wall behind the children's beds to be too hard and cold, so the lower part was covered with softboard. The beds are custom- made and the girls' beds could also be used as settees – for this purpose cushions were produced that were stored in built-in drawers. The beds also have fold up head- and foot boards to give the children a feeling of security as they lay in bed. Two small wall cupboards hang on the wall near the beds and these were brought from the former house. They were imported from the US by an Amsterdam furniture firm and appear in the catalogue of Sears department store. Worktops were made on each side of the table top in the sitting/dining area where the children could do their homework. With simple adjustable supports these could be placed in three positions: flat, tilted and folded down. In the edge to which the worktops were hinged were built-in inkpots, penholders and reading lights.

The son's room
with the bed
and alcove for
the washbasin.
On the white
section behind
the grand piano
a blue panel
hangs, used for
covering one of
the windows.

In the bathroom the bath from the previous house was built in between cupboards. The whole was closed off by a folding swingdoor. When this was opened out and the sliding door of the adjoining bedroom was pulled across there was a screened area with the bath.

The ground floor interior forms a whole with the rest of the house. In the hall next to the front door is a glazed recess with a small mailbox and underneath shelves for outdoor toys. A wardrobe is built into the recess of the study wall. The upstairs staircase begins in the hall with three steps and a small landing. The electricity meter and fuse box are mounted on the wall of the landing, which has a white marble front, and a small wall cupboard with drawers. On the cuboard was the telephone, and a small settee on the landing screens this off and provides a seat when making phone calls. Under the landing is storage space, while the stairs can be closed off with a sliding door. This has a simple yet clever device whereby the door opens with a movement of the finger, but it can be obstructed upstairs so that undesired persons are barred access to the upper floor.

The space intended for a garage became a workroom. The rear part of which has been separated off and has storage cupboards and a work surface with a washbasin; it was used among other things as a darkroom. The study has a work corner with a washbasin, another work corner with a low cupboard, bookshelves and a large folding table, plus a sitting area with a large built-in chair and folding table. The balcony above the exterior window and door frames has a double floor. The space between is closed off with sliding doors and was used for storage.

28 The kitchen has a sink with a granite work surface and cupboards underneath with sliding doors. Next to the sink was a dishwasher, a gift from the director of the Utrecht Electricity Company. Mounted above the sink is a long cupboard with sliding doors with glass on all sides, while in the early years immediately to the left of the hall door to the kitchen there was a zinc trough for washing clothes. This was made especially for the house and had double sides. The space between was filled with sawdust to keep the washing suds warm. Above the trough was a gas heater for hot water. The zinc trough was later replaced by an earthenware sink and under cupboard. On the same side as the domestic help's room is a black painted cooking recess with two stoves, pan racks and next to these cupboards with sliding drawers and shelving above. Next to the door of the adjoining room is where the dumbwaiter descends from the upper floor. The kitchen also has a fitted storage cupboard on which the window shutters were placed when not in use. This area was largely used as a workspace and the parts of it that could get dirty through contact with hands and feet are painted in black or blue.

A facility for accessing provisions delivered from outside was built on the outside wall of the kitchen entrance and consisted of various parts. A special smaller window was fixed into the tall window frame and closed, like all the others, with a window stay. However the stay of this small window could be operated in such a way that tradespeople were able to open the window from outside. They then found the order inside and placed the bread, milk or whatever on a drawn-up hatch. This spot is marked on the outside by a bright red arrow and a sign with instructions. A similar notice was placed on the small window. Whenever it was opened and there was no message or there was no-one in the kitchen, it meant Schröder and her domestic help were probably upstairs. They could then be reached via a speaking tube with a horn.

On the ground floor there were various kinds of floor covering in the different rooms. The hall and staircase landing had blue linoleum, while the stairs had white. The kitchen had brown linoleum from the previous house, the workroom yellow, the domestic help's room was grey, while the study had black and grey felt. The covering on the upper floor is a composite of black and white rubber, grey felt and red-painted floorboards, which Rietveld devised himself after everything else was ready and while Schröder was in Switzerland recovering from the move and the interior design decorating. It is the final flourish in the three-dimensional compositions of elements in the walls, floor and ceiling. Schröder thought it was bright and cheerful but was not happy with the way it dominated the manner in which the furniture could be arranged. Also the white rubber was easily soiled. The children jumped over the area so as not to dirty it when they came home from school. Schröder did not find Rietveld's covering so appealing that it outweighed all the inconvenience it caused her.

The floor covering – linoleum, felt and rubber – as well as the glass in the house are the only materials incorporated

The mouthpiece
of the speaking
tube.

into the colour scheme that have their own colouring. Every other material used, inside and out, concrete, plasterwork, iron and wood was painted. Because Rietveld wanted areas of red in the floor covering for Schröder and her son's rooms but was unable to find any material in pure red, he painted the floorboards red.

In designing this house Rietveld was able to formulate his own architectural idiom, which he was free to take to extremes as Truus Schröder stimulated him in this. The application of colour in space was an intrinsic component of his research. He later admitted to Schröder that he sometimes asked himself whether he had gone to far with the colour scheme, whether he had overstepped the boundary between architecture and painting.

The colours he chose: red, blue and yellow or white, black and various shades of grey, were rarely used in a purely decorative sense. They support the role of the planes and lines in the spatial composition. Sometimes they serve a practical function as in the kitchen.

The grey paintwork continues from the wall that adjoins the one on the side of the Prins Hendriklaan outside to the inside of the house. In the workroom on the ground floor it becomes a strip of colour across the lower part of the wall and continues into the cuboards at the back of the room, which also have the same colour. On the upper floor the same grey continues inside to the outside of the wall cupboards. In keeping with the floor covering the entire interior is brightly coloured. There are black areas of wall in the study, the kitchen, outside the WC on the upper floor and behind the children's beds. The study also has a black ceiling that gives the space an extremely subdued atmosphere. Part of the hall ceiling is lavender, while the chimney piece was also the same colour but was later painted ultramarine. In Schröder's and the girls' rooms parts of the walls are painted yellow. In the domestic help's room both walls and ceiling are in yellow as the room lacked sun. In the son's room the wall behind the unit and the upper part of the exterior wall are dark grey and certain parts of the hall walls are in a lighter tone. The remaining walls and ceilings are white. The ceiling rails of the sliding walls on the same floor are red, yellow and black. The cupboards and the sliding walls are alternatively white, black and grey, apart from the high cupboard in the girls' room which is yellow. The central heating elements are grey, white or yellow. The unit is mainly yellow with black and white as well as red, blue and grey accents. Smaller details throughout the interior are white, black or grey or are painted in primary colours. All the paintwork has an eggshell finish apart from the doorknobs and lower parts of the doors in the hall and kitchen, which have a high gloss finish in the same colour to save their getting dirty. In the kitchen the parts of doors and drawers that tend to show up marks are painted black or blue.

The son's room and sitting/dining area separated from the daughters' room and the landing.

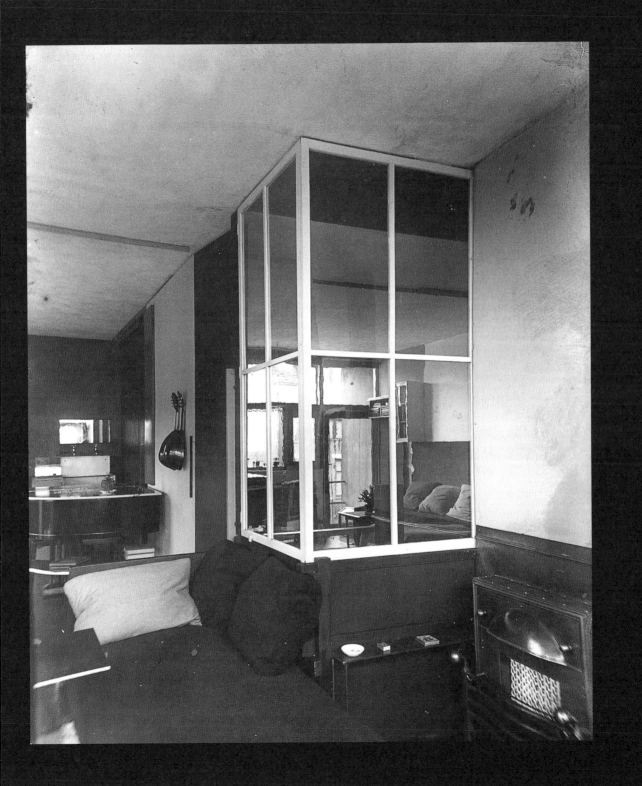

The sitting/din-
ing area sepa-
rated from the
rest of the upper
floor. The door
is still open.

The daughters'
room and the
landing sepa-
rated from the
bathroom, son's
room and sit-
ting/dining area.

Practical functioning

34　In the early years the house was used as it was conceived and designed. Thereafter changes were made to comply with the practicalities of day-to-day living, shifting ideas and a desire to experiment. When Rietveld began to work in line with the *Nieuwe Zakelijkheid* (new functionalist movement), the modular cupboard and floor covering on the upper floor disappeared as he felt he had overstepped the boundaries between architecture and painting and Schröder, herself, thought the covering too dominating. It was replaced with black ribbed rubber and linoleum. The large wooden sliding partition between the rooms of the children was difficult to operate because of its size and was sawn into two parts to make it less unwieldy. When the daughters had a friend who came to stay, who did not want to return home, and became part of the family for a year, an extra bed was added. To allow for this, the wooden beds were removed and two beds that folded out lengthwise were fitted into the wall. The underside of the springs was visible during the day, however, which looked less interesting than the designers envisaged and so it was quickly changed again. The ground floor workroom was used by Rietveld and Schröder as a studio for the former's budding architectural practice. In 1932 the studio was relocated to Oudegracht 55. In 1936 when the children had left home, Schröder wanted to live in a more compact way and so the kitchen was moved to her bedroom on the upper floor. The bathroom was redesigned at the same time. The enamelled iron bath was replaced by a granite hip bath designed by Rietveld in situ. The daughters' room was furnished as a bed- and workroom while the son's room became the guestroom. On the side of the built-in wardrobe a fold-out mirror was mounted. The light switch had to be moved to the inside of the cupboard to accommade this so the opening in the sliding wall was no longer needed. The kitchen downstairs became a bedsit and, like the workroom and the study, was rented out to tenants. This was necessitated as Schröder had poured her savings into dwellings across the road from her own, which she designed with Rietveld. In 1936 she lived there temporarily and the upper floor of her house was also let, first to a woman friend and later to a Montessori infant school.
Schröder and Rietveld's approach to the house was lighthearted and they made changes whenever they felt it necessary. When Schröder missed a place in her bedroom to store her combs, Rietveld made a sliding drawer under the washbasin by sawing out a section of the cupboard door underneath. He did not try to disguise it by painting the front of the drawer black like the cupboard door, but created a striking new look by painting the drawer blue and the inside yellow. When the kitchen downstairs was converted into a sitting room, the cupboard above the sink was sawn into pieces for firewood and stored under the staircase in the cellar. During restoration of the house they were found and provided valuable information for reconstructing the cupboard. During the war the neighbourhood was evacuated, but Schröder did not leave as she felt her house was too vulnerable to be vacated. At the time a munitions car had exploded near to the house blowing out all the windows. When the windows were replaced, the glass cupboard next to the front door was redesigned. The cupboard consists of two thick plates of glass with one protruding from the other

The house in use as a Montessori infant school.

The daughters' room with the sofa beds.

at the corners. Earlier on the plate was at right angles to the door but later was parallel to it.

Truus Schröder spent the rest of her life showing her house to those who were interested. Something she felt compelled to do in order to spread Rietveld's ideas on design. By 1935 the house drew so many visitors that she felt she no longer had any privacy in her own home. An extra room was then created on the roof where she could retreat. This was reached via a steel spiral staircase positioned above the stairs to the upper floor. When a retrospective of Rietveld's work was mounted in the Centraal Museum in Utrecht in 1958, Schröder had the room specially removed again. Around this period, Rietveld, following the death of his wife, went to live with Schröder until he died in 1964. He found the house complicated mainly because of the sliding walls. He was used to living more straightforwardly in his own house. However, he did once remark that he thought it a pleasant house nevertheless. Schröder died in 1985. She was placed on a bier in the ground-floor sitting room before being taken from the house to be buried.

The surroundings of the house changed dramatically over the years. Initially it was open on three sides in a position with magnificent views of the polder landscape on the outskirts of Utrecht. The impression of the inner and outer spaces flowing into each other was heightened by the fact that the polder land was considerably lower than the foundations of the house. It occupied only a small site, so Schröder rented land from the local council where the children could play. At the end of this she built a shed for storing outdoor playthings. This was on the side of Prins Hendriklaan and screened by a Rietveld-designed fence of round white wooden posts with black horizontal angle bars.

36

In 1964 the by-pass at right angles to Prins Hendriklaan was extended to a four-lane motorway that went over the avenue by way of a viaduct. This meant the house was cut off from the landscape it originally overlooked and lay now in a hollow as it were. Rietveld thought this diminished its spatial significance and he suggested pulling the house down. But the house remained and instead he had trees and shrubs planted around the house to protect it from everything going on around it. In 1952 a garage was built at the rear of the house according to Rietveld's design. This was originally intended as storage space but later, when Rietveld went to live with Schröder, it was used for his car. The garage floor is lower than the building's ground floor and is painted black in order to be as unobtrusive as possible. Around the house concrete paving was laid for the entrance, for sitting areas under the balconies and for paths between them and to the pavement on Prins Hendriklaan. Rietveld himself took a sledgehammer to the concrete paving of the paths to enable plants to grow between the resulting cracks. Greenery was also planted between the paved surfaces.

The house was restored in phases. The exterior was restored when the house was 50 years old in 1974 and became a listed building. Shortly after this, the garden and fencing was rehabilitated and after Schröder's death the interior was restored. In its time in 1924 the house uncompromisingly demonstrated a new form of architecture and a new manner of living, though this unmistakable feature was harder to distinguish through the changes made over the years. The restoration is aimed at clearly expressing the essence of its original appearance once again. This led to such key elements as the kitchen, beds, storage unit, wall cupboards, the tall standing cupboard between the childrens' rooms, the iron washbasins and the floor covering being completely reconstructed and the colours copied exactly.

The worktop of the sitting/dining area, folded out and folded down.

The sitting/dining area with the door to the balcony and, left of this, the dumbwaiter. Under the top for the dumbwaiter are steps used to reach the hatch in the glass roof structure.

The bedroom of Truus Schröder seen from the sitting/dining area.

The bathtub from the house in Biltstraat enclosed by cupboards. The space in front of the bath can be partitioned off using the double swing doors, visible to the left, and the sliding door between the bedroom and bathroom.

A fitted drawer for storing combs, later added, and made by sawing out a corner of the small cupboard door.

Ida van Zijl

The relevance of the Schröder house in Rietveld's work

In 1963, a year before Rietveld's death, the publication *Kwadraat Blad* (Quadrate Journal) ran an issue devoted to the Rietveld Schröder house.[1] The 35-page edition is illustrated with colour lithographs from the 1950s, Rietveld's drawings and sketches, a photograph inscribed 'Utrecht 1924' and five recent photographs of the house taken by *Kwadraat Blad*'s publisher Pieter Brattinga. The handwritten information about the illustrations is by Rietveld himself:

The building of this house is an attempt to break free of the humdrum excesses, which around 1920, after the honest styles of Berlage and other innovators, still influenced the architecture. We used solely primary forms, shapes and colours because these are so elementary and because they are free of association.

He explained this principle in more detail in an unpublished text from 1960:[2]

In order to separate space, form and colour from associations (in order to remain only on visual ground), more was needed than the search for immersing oneself externally into this: it was necessary to use the seeing itself as a starting point.

...

By exploring how visual impressions are composed of elementary perceptions, it is possible to work with space, form and colour elements that are so neutral that all association was ruled out. By working for a decade in this way (i.e. with primary forms, colours and spaces) a new appreciation of the visual can be constructed. One example of working according to this principle is Pr. Hendrikl. 50, the house that was created together with the interior designer T. Schröder.

The three dimensional in usage, construction and the visual image make the clarification of this spatial boundary possible, which almost nowhere results in enclosure.

The open and closed, the light and the massive, the indoor/outdoor are clearly arranged into a unified whole. The works following this were (for me) only possible after the liberation achieved through this work; which is not to say, of course, that others cannot arrive at innovation via an entirely different route.

It also not true to say that in so far as there is the question of an artistic expression in architecture, this can exist by working according to a principle – it is more the case that the principle formulates itself during or after the deed.

The Schröder house was a liberation for Rietveld in more than one sense. It rounded off the period in which he developed from a furniture maker, traditionally and professionally trained, into an avant-garde architect. After completing the house he set up his own architectural practice in a downstairs room overlooking the Prins Hendriklaan. His furniture workshop was taken over by his personal assistant G.A. van de Groenekan. Rietveld conquered not only the tedious excesses of existing architecture, but he was the first to succeed in translating the ideas of De Stijl into a concrete architectonical form. The house is the apotheosis of his contribution to this movement and also unique in his œuvre. In the designs he produced after 1924 De Stijl's influence is marginal. A direct similarity in form is only evident in the windows of the house he designed for M.J.L. Lommen (1925) and in the bedroom for An Harrenstein-Schräder,

Schröder's sister (1926). In the chauffer's flat for H. van der Vuurst de Vries (1927-28) his efforts were aimed at the industrialisation of building techniques and materials. At the time Rietveld discovered his affinity with the functionalist movement in architecture. In 1928, along with the Dutch architects H.P. Berlage and Mart Stam, he represented the Netherlands at the inauguration congress of the Congrès Internationaux d'Architecture Moderne (CIAM). The Schröder house represents a synthesis of every influence he had encountered together with the ideas he had developed in the preceding years. De Stijl played a large role in this development, but just as important were his contacts with the people in his immediate circle such as Bart van der Leck, Willem van Leusden and Truus Schröder.

1917-1924

Gerrit Thomas Rietveld was born on 24 June 1888 in Utrecht, the second son of a furniture maker. After primary school he learned the furniture making trade at his father's workshop. In 1917 he established his own furniture workshop on Adriaan van Ostadelaan 25 (later at 93), living with his family above the premises. He made his first revolutionary chair designs the following year: a wood and leather child's chair and a reclining chair from wooden planks. This burst of creativity followed a period of around 10 years in which he put his talents to the test in various fields. In particular the influence of artist friends had a defining impact on his artistic development. At the time Utrecht was a quiet provincial town, where a small group of people, who knew each other and were friends, followed cultural developments by way of the several artistic societies active in the city. The 16-year-old Rietveld learned of new movements in art and architecture through attending the evening classes of P.J.C. Klaarhamer. This Utrecht architect was a great admirer of H.P. Berlage (1856-1936) and Frank Lloyd Wright (1869-1959) and he had one or two interesting architectural designs to his credit. At the time Klaarhamer worked in collaboration with the painter Bart van der Leck (1876-1958). When Van der Leck moved to Laren in 1916, he became friendly with Piet Mondrian. Probably under Mondrian's influence, he switched to making abstractions of his figurative paintings. He gradually pared down realistic depiction to a composition of separate geometrical planes in primary colours on a white background.[3] In Rietveld's reclining chair, which is made of slats, a key design from 1918, he achieves a reduction in form that parallels the process of abstraction found in the work of Van der Leck.

Rietveld reduced the components of a traditional armchair to simple strips of wood and flat boards that were connected in such a way that they appeared to float in space. This starting point, primarily aimed at a spatial effect, basically distinguishes his chair from other avant-garde designs around this time. The simplifying of form, the lack of ornament and the use of what were termed honest and sober materials had already been explored by Mackintosh, Wright and Berlage. They were inspired, however, by the simplicity of pre-industrial handcrafted furniture and did not have the same visual departure points that Rietveld had in mind. The possibility of machine production, which Rietveld mentions in an accompanying explanation to an illustration of his work featured in an issue of De Stijl, as being the second most important aspect of modern design, was extremely important to him, although it was not an innate feature of this particular work.[4] Rietveld's early chair designs have a visual quality closely more aligned to developments in painting. Theo van Doesburg recognised a kindred spirit in Rietveld and it was for this reason that he published his work in De Stijl.

Between 1918 and 1924, Rietveld borrowed other formal aspects from painting. The most noticeable are the colours red, yellow and blue used in combination with black, white and grey. De Stijl painters restricted themselves to this palette in order to replace a realistic interpretation of nature with a universal abstraction of forms. In traditional architecture colour has a less highly associative significance. Rietveld used primary colours in order to heighten the autonomy of each element used to form his spatial compositions. In the Schröder House he thoroughly exploited the possibilities of this visual approach. However, such use of colour was not essential to his manner of working, and after 1924 was employed only sporadically.

The asymmetrical form, a second compositional element that Rietveld, under the influence De Stijl introduced into his work, was to remain a characteristic feature. The collaboration with people in his immediate circle was also of decisive significance.

In 1922, together with the painter Willem van Leusden, Rietveld designed the interior and furniture for the waiting room of Dr Hartog in Maarssen. The chairs and cupboards are variations of his furniture style using strips of wood. The tubes of the hanging lamp are organised in a similar manner to the planes and lines of his furniture, but now as an asymmetrical composition. Van Leusden conceived the colours for the furniture and it is likely that Rietveld introduced him to other De Stijl members. Van Leusden converted for a while to architecture and created three models that were shown at De Stijl exhibition in Galerie Rosenberg in Paris. *The Urinal/Transformer Station* by Van Leusden from 1922 is the earliest design that clearly illustrates the architectonic principles of De Stijl. The asymmetrical shape consists of alternate open and closed planes in which the walls and canopies protrude beyond the tangents. Van Doesburg often reproduced this work in his articles on the development of modern architecture in the Netherlands.[5]

There is a striking visual similarity between this model and the furniture for *Space-Colour-Composition*, an interior Rietveld designed with Vilmos Huszár in 1923 for the *Juryfreie Kunstschau* in Berlin. Opinion varies on Rietveld's contribution to this. Moreover it is unclear whether this interior was actually ever realised. The so-called Berlin chair, however, is certainly from Rietveld's hand. In this design he consciously used an asymmetrical construction. The containment implicit in a symmetrical form was therefore 'broken' open. Just as important was his use of wooden planks for each part of the chair. The difference between frame, seat and support, still present in his furniture made from strips of wood, have disappeared. The entire chair consists of flat planes and by arranging these asymmetrically and having them lengthened in front or behind, above or under each other, the chair becomes a sculptural form that accentuates the surrounding space.

In 1923 Rietveld also made models from the architectural designs that Theo van Doesburg and Cornelis van Eesteren wanted to show at an exhibition of De Stijl in Galerie Rosenberg. By taking various routes, Rietveld acquired an idiom of his own that enabled him to give expression to a form of architecture aimed at the experiencing of space. From that moment the visual means for building the Rietveld Schröder house lay within his grasp.

Truus Schröder (1889-1985)

Rietveld employed his visual design idiom to maximum effect in the house for Mrs Schröder-Schräder, though in this case the role of the client was also crucial to the design process.

Truus Schröder was born in Deventer in 1889. Following her training and a short period abroad, she returned to the Netherlands and in 1911 married Frits Schröder, a lawyer from Utrecht. The course in architecture she had intended to follow was therefore abandoned.

Their differences in character and outlook did not make for an easy marriage, though there was understanding on both sides. This is evident from Frits Schröder's suggestion that his wife design a room according to her own ideas in their 19th century house on Biltstraat. The choice fell on the young Rietveld, whom they knew through Cornelis Begeer, one of Schröder's clients. Truus Schröder liked Rietveld's design for the remodelling of Begeer's Gold and Silversmith Company. After designing her room, Rietveld and Schröder stayed in touch. Rietveld showed her room to various friends and colleagues, which must have been extremely stimulating for Schröder, since she had a particular interest in architecture.

Schröder's wishes for her new house were closely linked to her personal situation and social outlook. She wished to free herself from what she experienced as the stifling milieu of her late husband, and was seeking more intimacy and a feeling of security for her and her children. Her desire for freedom and openness is shown in the open-plan layout of the upper floor of her house where light streams in from all sides, and in the five entrance doors downstairs giving every room its own access to outside. The sense of security is manifest in the choice of siting the main living space on the upper floor, somewhat removed from the eyes of the outside world, and in the fact that it could be partitioned into smaller spaces by using sliding walls.

Schröder was also interested in current feminist views on housekeeping. An authority in this field was the American Christine Frederick, who published *The New Housekeeping. Efficiency Studies in Home Management* in 1913 in which Taylorian ideas on the rationalisation of production processes were translated in terms of housekeeping.[6] Her ideas had been enthusiastically received in Germany, the influence of which can be found in the booklet *Die Neue Wohnung* by Bruno Taut. The third reprint, published at the end of 1924, was given the subtitle *Die Frau als Schöpferin* and Schröder owned a copy.[7] She knew Taut personally as he was among those to whom Rietveld had shown her room on Biltstraat. From the contents and the many passages underlined it is obvious how strikingly similar her views were to those in the booklet. In her house these ideas are mainly to be found in the kitchen. Written on one of the rare design sketches are elaborate notes on the practical layout for this space. Among the many practical details, such as the adjustable shelving by the windows, the client's contribution is clearly discernible.

In the Rietveld Schröder House various social and cultural developments from the first decades of the 20th century are drawn together. Rietveld absorbed these influences through direct contact with those in his own circle: Bart van der Leck, Willem van Leusden and Truus Schröder. To their input, he added his own inimitable and intuitive feeling for space. As Bertus Mulder once said: 'Rietveld was able to make something that completely expressed his own ideas, while conforming to the wishes of his client.'[8]

1 The *Kwadraat-Blad* (Quadrate Journal) was a publication from the printing company steendrukkerij de Jong & Co, which was printed in a limited circulation of 2,000 and mailed to friends and business associates. It was compiled and edited by Pieter Brattinga. In 1985 the Reflex publishing house in Utrecht reprinted this issue. 2 NAi, Rietveld-archief nr. 752. 3 C. Hilhorst, Bart van der Leck. In: *De beginjaren van De Stijl* (The early years of De Stijl), Utrecht 1982, p.167. 4 *De Stijl* vol.2 (1919), no.11, p.439. 5 D. Adelaar et al, *Willem van Leusden*, Utrecht 1990, p.93. 6 Details from C. Nagtegaal, *Tr. Schröder-Schräder. Bewoonster van het Rietveld Schröderhuis*, Utrecht 1987. 7 M. Boot et al, '*De rationele' keuken in Nederland en Duitsland. Achtergronden en ontwikkelingen en consequenties voor (huis)vrouwen.*' In: *Berlijn-Amsterdam 1920-1940 Wisselwerkingen*, Amsterdam 1982, pp. 339-347. 8 Facts for this article, unless stated otherwise, were taken from M. Küper/I. van Zijl's *Gerrit Rietveld 1888-1964. Het volledige werk.* Utrecht 1992.

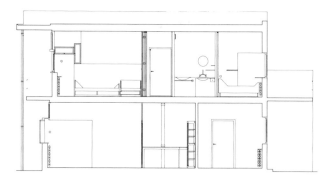

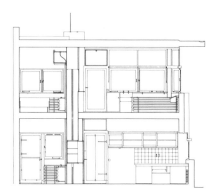

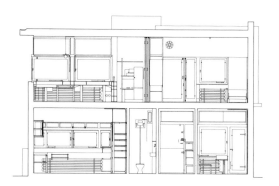

Interior, south-
westfront.

Interior, north-
westfront.

Interior, north-
eastfront.

Interior, south-
eastfront.

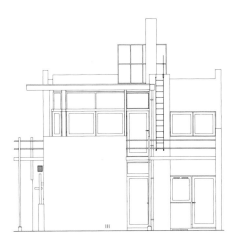

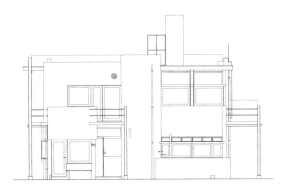

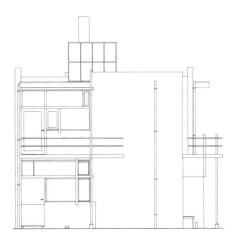

Exterior, north-
eastfront.

Exterior, south-
eastfront.

Interior, south-
westfront.

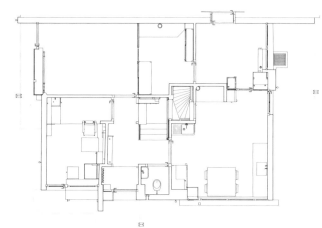

Upper floor
layout with
partitions
closed.

Ground floor
layout.

Upper floor
layout with
partitions open.